SKILLMINDS PRESS

How to keep from being a victim of a home burglary

5 Simple common sense tips that will save your belongings

Contents

1

Introduction

One of the worst crimes that people become a victim of is a burglary at your home. The home is the place that all of us are supposed to feel safe and secure. So when someone invades that space it is an awful feeling. If you've ever been a victim of a burglary, then you know that feeling. Sometimes we become complacent with ourselves and our property because we think, "Oh it will never happen to me". Well there is a burglary every 30 seconds in the United States, which means there are two burglaries every minute. So you do the math on how many victims there will be at the end of the day or the week.

My name is JT, I am a retired police officer with 27 years of experience. In my career, I have seen many many burglaries that could have been avoided with some simple things that take seconds to check or do before you leave your house. This book will give you five tips that might seem like it's just common sense, but sometimes we neglect to do them and all it takes is just one time to forget and you become a victim.

Burglars look for a variety of things when they are planning to break into a home. You can say that this crime is not necessarily a crime of opportunity like someone breaking into your car or someone stealing your packages from your front porch, but several factors do come into play. Burglars look for a variety of things, such as lighting, large numbers of newspapers on the lawn (if you still subscribe to the paper), empty driveways, open backyard gates or anything to indicate that no one is home. Now I'm not saying that all burglaries occur with these indicators, but a good percentage has several factors that let burglars know that your home is a prime target.

So you might say to yourself, well what am i to do, I have to go to work and my house is alone for at least eight hours a day. Now if your household is like many others, both parents work and the kids are either at school or with friends. There are several things that you can do that will give you a better chance of NOT becoming a victim. So let's explore what we can do.

2

Securing Entry Points

Tip #1 - "Locking your House"

In today's busy world we leave our house in a hurry and expect that our house will eventually be locked when the last person leaves. Well that could work well if everyone left through the same door. How many times have you been the first one home and found the back door open or side door open? It happens more than what we want to believe. Or you get home and the garage door is open. Do we find out how this happens or do we just check everything is in order and let it slide. Remember a simple leaf can blow in as the garage door is closing and trigger the sensors which automatically opens the door. It just takes a few more seconds to make sure your garage door is closed completely. It is very important that you make sure all entry points are locked and secure. Doors and windows are common entry points for burglars. If left unsecured, it just makes it that much easier for a burglar to make you a victim. You should remain vigilant in the security of your home and never become complacent.

Most of us have regular schedules that we follow day in and day out. Burglars look for such routines to avoid getting caught. They look for what time you take off to drop off the kids at school, how long it takes you to come back or if you stop at the local restaurant for the morning coffee. Don't be a creature of habit. Vary your schedules as much as you can so anyone watching to see what you do, will never know when you're home. A simple thing like leaving the television or radio on while you make your errands can help keep burglars unsure if they come knocking at your door.

We never think that an unlocked door can become an issue when the police officer taking the report looks for any type of forced entry into the home and cannot find one. This should be a constant practice before anyone leaves the home. Make sure that all entry points are secured except the one that will be used to leave the house.. If you have a pet and you take him out in the morning through the back door or any door, make sure you lock it when you let him back in. This way, if no one else uses that door, no one has to remember to lock it before everyone leaves for their daily routines.

You can also choose to upgrade your doors and locks. A weak door will not help keep a burglar out. Even adding a deadbolt, if you don't have one, will help in making the door a little more secure. If you recently moved into your home or lost your house keys, a good practice to follow is to replace the locks altogether. You can upgrade your door locks to an electronic smart lock. These locks will lock themselves after a couple of minutes after being opened and they can also be accessed through an application. It can be checked if your door is properly secure from anywhere you are. Even if you're running to the corner store or dropping off the kids at school, you need to lock your door. Burglars check for unlocked doors after they ring or knock to see if anyone is home. The days of hiding the key under the mat or a fake rock are gone. There is no excuse why you would not lock all entry points.

The same goes for the garage, it can be checked through an app if it is locked or not, but we fail to double check it and the door remains open inviting burglars. Keeping our homes secure should be a routine. Creating a routine to lock our home, will make it easier in preventing your home being burglarized.

3

Window Security

Tip #2 - "Lock your windows"

Something that would go hand in hand with tip #1, but is worth mentioning by itself, is locking your windows. Sometimes we assume because they are closed, they are locked. An open window is a very common and vulnerable place for a burglar to gain access into your home and just leave out the back door.

A locked window might not keep the burglar from breaking it, but the less attention that they attract to what they are doing, the better for them. Some homes have shatter proof glass, but an unlocked window is an entryway no matter if it is made of steel.

So this also becomes something that we must do as a common routine. Now don't think that because you have a two story house you can leave the upstairs open. Unless you reside in a high rise building, it's best if you lock the upstairs as well. Burglars will use ladders and tools that are left unsecured on your property to gain access to your home. A locked backyard gate might not be a bad idea also. You don't want to leave anything to chance.

There are several types of window locks on the market. You should choose one that works with the type of window you have at your home. For example, a sliding back door comes with the regular switch up or down to unlock the door. Now you can buy an expensive lock for the door, but did you know that a simple broom stick, cut to the length of the opposite glass door and laid on the sliding channel will prevent the sliding door from opening? The burglar would have to break the glass which will attract attention to himself. Some homeowners choose to install window steel bars for extra security, but curtains, blinds or window film also offer a good deterrent from someone looking inside your home. If they can't see in, the curiosity to get in will diminish in comparison to looking inside your home and seeing your valuables ready for the taking.

We all love a beautiful garden with big hedges or large plants that will give us privacy. But something to keep in mind is that burglars will also use that to their advantage. So it is also a good idea to trim your hedges and plants that might cover any window low enough to keep any burglar from hiding behind them. The increased visibility will help avoid burglars from entering your home under the cover of plants.

4

Alarm System

Tip #3 - "Home Alarm"

Most homes today are wired with a home security system. If not, you can pick up a wireless system at a fair price with your local electronics store. But even if you have a million dollar system, it is no good if it is not the system is not armed. The system is only good if it is set to do what it's supposed to do, which is alert the police if someone enters your home WHILE IT IS ARMED.

Something to also take into account is that the more visible the alarm system is, the better it is for you because it relays a message to any would-be burglar, that your home is protected and it is not an easy target. You want to make sure your main entryways are visible by your cameras to catch any suspicious activity. Some cameras sound an alert when movement is detected to let you know that it is recording. Most alarm systems come with motion and door/window sensors as well as monitoring and notification services. Regular testing and maintenance, as well as integrating smart home security devices is recommended.

If your budget does not allow for a security system, you can purchase fake cameras and place them around your home. No one knows whether it is a working camera or not. The idea here is to deter any intruders or would-be burglars from choosing your home as a target.

The use of timers can also be a deterrent against having your home burglarized because it makes it look like someone is home. Even though FBI statistics indicate that a higher percentage of burglaries occur during the day and not under the cover of darkness. It is always a good idea to use the timers to where they will turn on your lights at different times of the day or evening in case your families routine carries over to the evening hours.

5

Community Involvement

Tip #4 - "Use your Neighbors"

How many of you actually know your neighbors? I can't even count the times that I responded to a crime scene where we had to talk to the neighbors for further information and found that no one knew each other. Except for the gender and what vehicle the victim drove.

Getting to know the neighbors is actually a very good idea, not only because we live next to each other, but also because we can watch out for each other when needed. Now I'm not saying you have to be nosy, but it might someday help out, you just never know.

Start a neighborhood watch program. What is that? It is simply a group of people that live in the same area and watch out for each other to make their neighborhood as safe as possible. The more people that are involved, the safer your neighborhood will be. It does not take much to start one. The first thing you need is a person to organize the neighbors. Announce what you want to do and what benefits it will bring to your neighborhood.

Once your neighbors are on board with the idea, contact your local law enforcement to coordinate a time to meet. Invite the police to the neighborhood where it's easier and convenient for the group to meet. This is a very important part of your neighborhood watch because the group will create an alliance with the police department, thus building a stronger community network. The police department will advise the group of all the do's and don'ts of the neighborhood watch program as well as the group can express any concerns they might have. If the department has a Crime Stoppers program, they can also help in obtaining signs that will announce that a neighborhood watch is in effect in the area. Again, trying to deter any type of criminal activity.

THIS IS A
NEIGHBOURHOOD
WATCH
AREA

The group can hold regular monthly meetings to keep everyone informed and or share information of any recent incidents. In between such meetings, the group can communicate with each other through social media or applications such as "Nextdoor". This will keep the group informed of any suspicious activity. So if you see something, then say something. The idea is to keep your home and property secure. Neighborhood Watch programs play an important part in deterring burglaries by promoting a sense of group responsibility.

6

Social Media Awareness

Tip #5 - Social Media Usage

We all enjoy our vacations and showing our friends and family how much fun we are having. The only problem with this is that burglars also look through social media for those beautiful times that you are having. Of course this means to them that your house is available to be burglarized. This is where social media and home security intersect. An announcement that you will be traveling on such and such date and won't be returning until two weeks later is asking to become a victim of a burglary. Unless you have done your due diligence in making sure your home is as secure as possible, then by all means, publicize your vacation, but you're just asking for trouble. A more sensible way to share your vacation would be upon your return and I'm sure everyone will enjoy your pics just as well.

The things to avoid on social media is location sharing and your complete travel plans, but you can share general advice with the community, success stories and preventive measures.

Social media can play as a double edge sword. It is a great tool for communication and information, but if we use it the wrong way, it can be used against us. Facebook is the most used social media, totaling over 3 billion users per quarter. It is followed closely by Tik Tok and Twitter. In other words don't announce your whereabouts until you get back home.

7

Conclusion

In conclusion, safeguarding your home involves a multi-faceted approach that addresses various vulnerabilities. First, always remember to lock your house securely, including doors and windows, as this serves as the fundamental defense against burglaries. Investing in home alarm systems adds an extra layer of protection, acting as a deterrent and providing timely alerts. Community involvement fosters a sense of collective security, encouraging neighbors to look out for one another. Be aware of strangers that you come across or service providers that you allow inside your home. Finally, be cautious about sharing detailed information on social media, as oversharing can inadvertently provide potential burglars with insights into your daily routines and the vulnerability of your home. By adopting these five key practices, you can significantly reduce the risk of home burglaries and create a safer living environment for yourself, your family and your community. Be proactive and not reactive!

8

Resources

Burglary rate by state U.S. 2022 | Statista. (2023, November 6). Statista. https://www.statista.com/statistics/232580/burglary-rate-in-the-us-by-state/

Ebert, J. (2021, September 11). *Burglary – how to prevent it, and the mistakes that invite thieves into our homes.* homesandgardens.com. https://www.homesandgardens.com/advice/how-to-prevent-burglary

Edwards, R. (2023, May 5). *8 Surprising home burglary facts and Stats.* SafeWise. https://www.safewise.com/blog/8-surprising-home-burglary-statistics/

Gabriele, R. (2023, May 31). *2023 Crime rates in U.S. cities report.* SafeHome.org. https://www.safehome.org/resources/crime-statistics-by-state/

How to start a neighborhood watch group in 5 easy steps | National Neighborhood Watch. (n.d.). Blue Water Media. https://www.nnw.org/start

Neighborhood Watch and social Media | National Neighborhood Watch. (n.d.). Blue Water Media. https://nnw.org/neighborhood-watch-and-social-media

www.ingramcontent.com/pod-product-compliance
Lightning Source LLC
Chambersburg PA
CBHW070241260726
48658CB00006BA/2386